D1455813

SEALS

Tom Jackson

Grolier
an imprint of

www.scholastic.com/librarypublishing

Published 2008 by Grolier
An imprint of Scholastic Library Publishing
Old Sherman Turnpike, Danbury,
Connecticut 06816

For The Brown Reference Group plc
Project Editor: Jolyon Goddard
Copy-editors: Lesley Ellis, Lisa Hughes,
    Wendy Horobin
Picture Researcher: Clare Newman
Designers: Jeni Child, Lynne Ross,
    Sarah Williams
Managing Editor: Bridget Giles

Volume ISBN-13: 978-0-7172-6243-4
Volume ISBN-10: 0-7172-6243-X

**Library of Congress
Cataloging-in-Publication Data**

Nature's children. Set 1.
    p. cm.
  Includes index.
  ISBN-13: 978-0-7172-8080-3
  ISBN-10: 0-7172-8080-2
  1. Animals--Encyclopedias, Juvenile.
  QL49.N38 2007
  590--dc22

                2007018358

Printed and bound in China

Contents

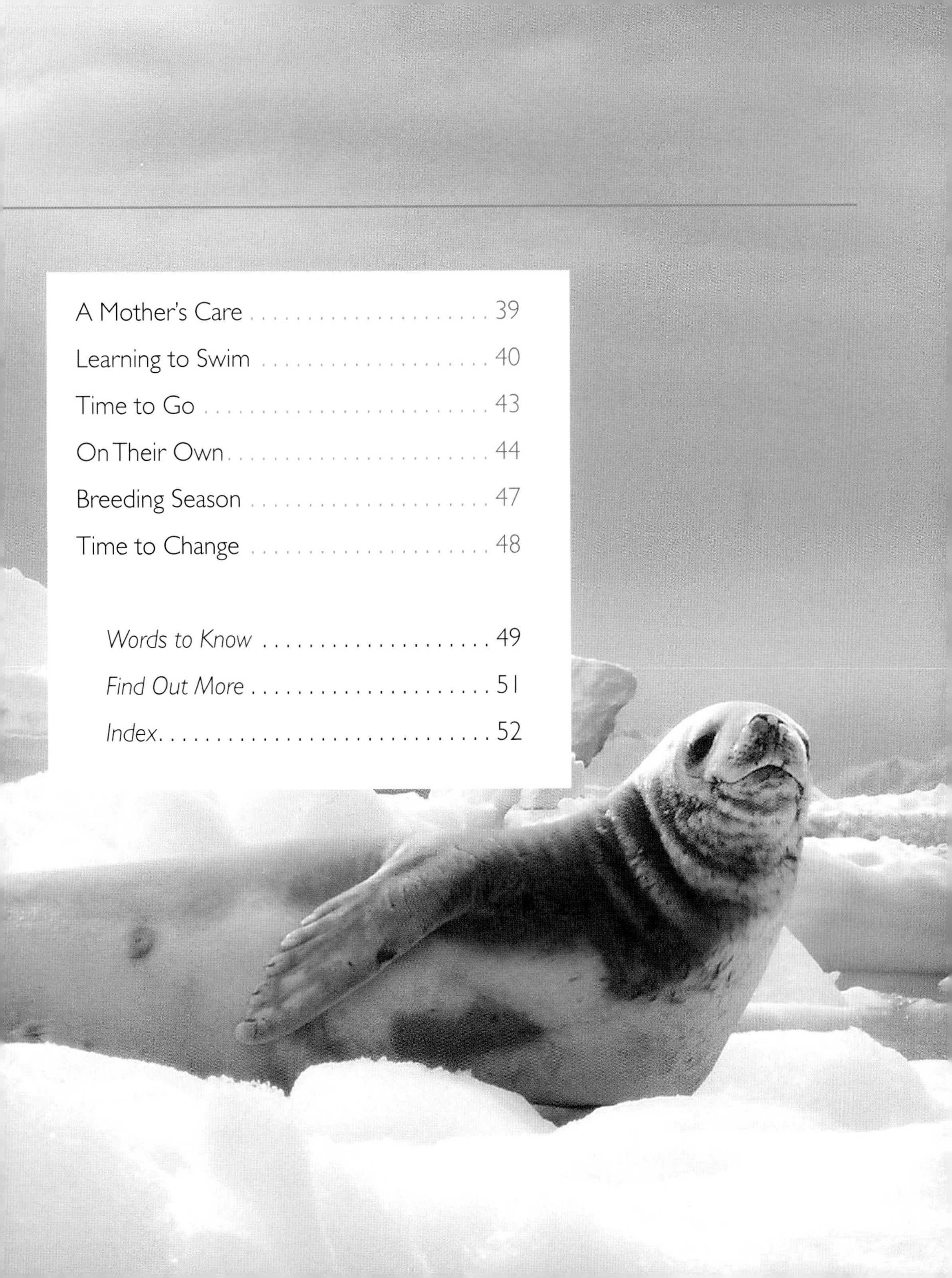

FACT FILE: Seals

Class	Mammals (Mammalia)
Order	Carnivores (Carnivora)
Family	Earless seals (Phocidae)
Genera	13 genera around the world
Species	18 species living worldwide. Common species around the coasts of North America are harbor seal, harp seal, and elephant seal
World distribution	Most seals live in cold water around the north and south poles. However, some live along the coasts of North America. A few species live in much warmer places
Habitat	Seals spend most of the year in the sea, but they come onto land or ice to give birth
Distinctive physical characteristics	Seals do not have ears, just openings in the sides of the head. Their back legs are flippers that can only point backward
Diet	Mainly fish; some eat penguins and shellfish

Introduction

What swims like a fish and barks like a dog?
If you guessed "a seal," you're right! These
whiskery sea mammals are distantly related
to dogs, although one of the few things they
have in common today is their bark.

Seals, unlike most dogs, are expert swimmers
and can twist and turn through the water at
great speed. They can also dive out of sight into
very deep water. On land, seals are not quite as
graceful, but they like to come onto beaches to
meet other seals or to just rest in the sun.

**A leopard seal
has a typical seal
body shape.**

A seal's arm is a flat flipper. Flippers aren't much use on land but are excellent for swimming.

6

Fins for Feet

Seals belong to a group of animals called the **pinnipeds**. This name means "fin-footed," and it is obvious why seals belong to this group. Instead of arms and legs, seals have flat flippers shaped like paddles. These flippers might make it hard for the seals to walk on land, but they are very useful for swimming in water.

Seals are just one type of pinniped. True seals are also called earless seals, so people can easily tell them apart from the other pinnipeds. The other pinnipeds are walruses and eared seals. Eared seals are also called sea lions or fur seals. More than half of all pinnipeds are earless seals, and about half of those live in the seas around North America.

Seal or Sea Lion?

Many people think that seals and sea lions are the same things. But once you know how to tell them apart, it is easy to see which is which. The most obvious difference is the ears. True seals do not have any external ears, but sea lions do. That is why **zoologists** call sea lions eared seals. Fur seals also have ears and are relatives of sea lions.

The other big difference between true seals and sea lions is their back legs. Sea lions and fur seals can stand on their hind legs, even though they are flattened into flippers for swimming. The sea lions waddle about on their legs while on land. True seals are different. Their hind feet are also flattened into flippers, but true seals cannot stand up on their hind legs. In the water, sea lions paddle with their front flippers and steer with the back ones. True seals use their back flippers as a big fin to do most of the swimming work. Their front flippers are small and are tucked against the body while swimming.

Unlike true seals,
a sea lion has visible
ears and can stand
on its hind flippers.

The elephant seal is the largest member of the seal family.

All Sizes of Seals

The smallest seal is the ringed seal, which lives around North America and in most cold parts of the northern hemisphere. Ringed seals are about 5 feet (1.5 m) long and weigh up to 310 pounds (140 kg).

The largest seals are the elephant seals. The northern elephant seal lives along the west coast of North America. Elephant seals can grow to 17 feet (5 m) long and weigh 6,000 pounds (2.7 metric tons). That is heavier than a small pickup truck! As well as being the largest seals, elephant seals are among the largest animals in the world. The male, or **bull**, elephant seals are bigger than the female, or **cow**, elephant seals. In some cases, a bull may be six times the size of a cow. Adult bulls are easily recognizable by their huge nose that looks like an elephant's trunk. Female elephant seals and young males do not have this "trunk."

Ocean and Land

Seals are mammals, so they are related to sheep, cats, and even humans, like you. All mammals have hairy bodies and breathe air, and feed their young milk. Most of them live on land. A few mammals, such as whales and dolphins, never come onto land. However, seals are one of the few mammals that split their time between the ocean and the land. They are just as comfortable swimming far out to sea as they are basking in the sun on a beach.

Seals are not very fussy about where they call home. They are content on the rocky shores of Maine or on a sandy beach in California. In the far north, where the sea is so cold it freezes, seals do not even need a beach. They climb out of the water to float on the ice. Some seals swim into river mouths, where the water is not salty. One species, the Baikal seal, lives in a huge freshwater lake in the middle of Russia!

A leopard seal
rests on ice.

When diving, seals can hold their breath for up to 20 minutes.

Deep Breathing

A seal is built for swimming. Its streamlined body lets it slide through the water easily and dive to the seafloor. However, even the best swimmers have to come up to the surface to breathe. Most people can hold their breath underwater for a few seconds or a minute. A seal can stay underwater for 20 minutes!

Like nearly all living things, a seal needs **oxygen** to live. It gets this oxygen by breathing air. Before a seal dips below the water's surface, it inhales, or breathes in, and then exhales, or blows out, all the air in its lungs. Empty lungs make it easier to swim to great depths.

The oxygen from its last inhale goes into the seal's blood, just as it does when you breathe in. However, a seal's body uses that oxygen more efficiently than a person's does. A seal can stay underwater for much longer than a person. That's because while the seal is diving, oxygen goes to the most important organs in the seal's body, such as the heart and brain.

Deep-sea Divers

People have invented many clever machines that let us dive underwater and swim with seals and other sea life. But even so, we can only visit their world for a short time. Seals are just so much better at diving underwater than humans. Without any diving equipment, a human can only dive to about 150 feet (45 m). Going any deeper is very dangerous. Seals can dive to at least twice that depth. Some, such as the elephant seal, can go down to depths of 3,280 feet (1,000 m).

When a seal swims into the deep, its heart rate slows down so it can save energy. On the surface, its heart beats about 120 times a minute. However, once the seal is underwater, the heart rate slows to 40 to 60 beats per minute. On the longest and deepest dives, an elephant seal's heart beats only four to eight times a minute!

When a leopard seal dives, its heart rate slows to save energy.

An elephant seal's eyes can see well both underwater and out of water.

Eye Protection

A seal's large, brown eyes are not just beautiful, they are also very good at seeing underwater. Seals often swim in dark water, under ice, or so deep that only a little sunlight gets down that far. In the dark, the pupils at the center of the seal's eyes open very wide. Even the dimmest light can be picked up by such wide eyes. Back at the surface, the sensitive eyes need to be protected from the bright sunlight, so the pupils shrink to a tiny slit.

If you have ever gone swimming in the ocean, you will know that the saltwater can make your eyes sting. The best way to avoid that is to swim with your eyes shut, which is not very easy to do. A seal's eyes do not get sore. They are protected by an extra eyelid. This eyelid is see-through. It sweeps backward and forward over the eye when the seal goes underwater, washing the eyeball with tears. Tear fluid prevents saltwater from damaging the eye.

Blubber Blanket

How does a seal survive in freezing cold water? Luckily, it has a thick layer of fat, called **blubber**, under its skin. The blubber acts like a cozy blanket that keeps the seal's body heat from escaping its body. A seal's blubber is so effective that some seals spend their whole life swimming in freezing seas surrounded by blocks of ice!

Blubber also acts like the seal's life preserver. Blubber is very light, so it helps the seal stay afloat. The blubber can save the seal in another way, too. Sometimes, seals have to go without food for weeks at a time. Instead of going hungry, seals can live on the energy stored in their blubber.

A seal's thick layer of blubber keeps it warm in very cold climates.

If these young elephant seals get too hot while sunbathing, their flippers will help cool them.

Cool Flippers!

Seals may be good at staying warm, but what happens when they get too hot? Their blubber is so thick that even a short sunbathe on a hot beach can make a seal overheated. Seals cannot take off their blanket of blubber, so they have to get rid of the extra body heat in another way. They use their flippers.

A seal's flippers do not have any blubber on them. Instead there are many blood vessels under the skin. When it gets hot, a seal pumps more blood into the vessels in the flippers. The warm blood is cooled by the water or air surrounding the flippers. So heat escapes from the seal into the air. The cooled blood then travels back into the body, and soon the seal is at a more comfortable temperature.

Life and Death

Scientists can tell how old a tree is by counting the rings inside its trunk. Each year a new ring is added. The same is true of a seal's teeth and claws. By counting the layers in the animals' teeth and claws, scientists have discovered that some seals live for more than 40 years. However, most seals live for only about 25 years.

Wild seals rarely die of old age. Many are killed by disease or accidents. Most seals are killed by **predators**. A seal's main enemies are killer whales, polar bears, and sharks. Seal **pups** are killed by eagles and arctic foxes. Humans are also a threat to seals: fishers kill many pups each year because they believe the seals eat too many fish. Hunters kill adult seals for meat and oil, and pups for their fur.

Feeding Time

Seals always hunt in water. After all, they would not be able to catch much by wriggling around on land. Seals eat a lot of fish. The seals chase fish through the water, twisting and turning to catch them as they try to dart away. A seal's sensitive whiskers can pick up the tiny currents of water made by fish as they swim. So, seals can still find their prey in dark or muddy water.

Seals do eat many other foods, though. Harbor seals search tidepools for crabs. Harp seals hunt far out to sea and scoop up mouthfuls of shrimp and shrimplike shellfish called **krill**.

Many types of seals search for food on the seabed. Bearded seals have very long whiskers for feeling along the bottom for octopuses or sea snails. If seals find something, they dig it up using the claws on their front flippers. The seals crunch up shellfish and suck out the soft body. Then they spit out the bits of shell.

A leopard seal
barks to scare
away predators.

Finding a Friend

It is difficult for us to tell one seal from another. Their faces all look the same. Seals also find it hard. When they are crowded together on a beach, they cannot pick out the face of a friend among all the strangers. Seals cannot even see the differences between their own babies and those of the other seals.

Seals may not be able to see the differences, but they can definitely smell them. Seals have a very good sense of smell, and they use it to identify their relatives and friends. Although they might smell pretty much the same to us, each seal has a unique odor. A seal's nose is sensitive enough to recognize another seal just by the way it smells.

Seals use sound to communicate with one another. When seals meet, they call to each other using a range of noises, such as grunts, yelps, snorts, and squeaks. They also growl and bark at enemies. Mothers and babies use special calls to help them find each other on the beach.

Elephant seals
communicate
with one another
using sound.

Young elephant seals
like to hang out
together on beaches.

Alone or Together?

If you wanted to see seals, your best bet would be to look for a beach where they gather. However, seals spend most of their lives far away out at sea, coming on land only occasionally to rest.

Cows often gather together on the shore to raise their pups. Cows are pregnant for 11 to 12 months. They give birth to a single pup; twins are rare. The pups remain on land until they are old enough to swim. Depending on the type of seal, that might be a few days to ten weeks. The cows then head back to sea to breed again.

Some seals stay together out at sea. Harp seals live their whole lives in large groups, or herds. A herd of harp seals may contain thousands of seals. However, many other seals live alone. The ringed seal is an extreme example. Unlike other seals, ringed seals do not even meet up to give birth. Instead the pups are born in caves dug into the ice. The caves hide the pups from predators and protect them against the cold arctic wind. The only time adult ringed seals meet one another is the short time they spend looking for mates.

On the Move

Some birds fly south for winter and then come back again in summer. This type of journey is called a **migration**. Some seals migrate, too. For example, harp seals live in the **Arctic** and have to migrate to find food each winter. Harp seals hunt for fish along the edge of the ice sheet that covers the Arctic Ocean. In summer, when it is warm, much of the ice has melted. The harp seals travel in a herd to the far north, where it is still cold enough to have ice, to feed there.

As the weather gets colder in fall, more of the sea becomes frozen, and the ice sheet grows southward. The harp seals move with the ice and end up spending winter hundreds of miles away from where they were in summer. In spring, the ice sheet melts away, and the seals migrate north again, ending up back where they were the previous summer.

Two harp seals
come up to have
a look around.

Hawaiian monk seals don't have a breeding season, so pups may be born at any time of the year.

Birthdays

Seal mothers that live in places where it is always warm give birth to the babies at any time of year. That is what Hawaiian monk seals do. However, most seals live in places that have long, cold winters, when it would be hard to look after a baby. Most baby seals, or pups, are born at the end of winter, just when spring is around the corner. That way a mother knows there will be plenty of food for her pup when it heads off for its first hunt.

All seals give birth out of water. They haul themselves onto land or an **ice floe** to give birth because their pups cannot swim right away. The bulls do not help the cows give birth or look after the pups. However, the bulls stay close by because they want to **mate** with the cows and make next year's pups.

Seal Pups

Just like newborn humans, seal pups are much smaller than their parents. Some pups are bigger than others, though. A ringed seal pup weighs just 10 pounds (4.5 kg), whereas a baby bearded seal weighs 80 pounds (36 kg).

Pups that are born on ice have a white coat of woolly fur. The thick fur keeps the little seal warm while it builds up a layer of blubber like its mother's. The white coat also helps the pup stay out of sight of predators, which search the white snow for a bite to eat. Seals that are born on rocks or sand have a dark, **mottled** coat so they can stay hidden, too.

Harp seal pups are born on land. They have white fur that matches their icy surroundings.

37

A harp seal pup suckles milk from its mother.

A Mother's Care

Just like any baby, a seal pup is always hungry. It starts to feed on its mother's milk a few minutes after being born. Pups generally **nurse** on land or ice, but some do it while swimming with their mother. Seal milk is much fattier than human milk or that made by cows. In fact, seal milk is more like soft butter. The fat in the milk is used to make the pup's blubber.

A seal pup nurses for just a few weeks before it is left to look after itself. Although she is not with her pup for very long, a seal mother takes good care of her pup. The mother never goes far away for long and always makes sure the pup is out of danger.

Learning to Swim

Can you remember learning to swim? The water can be a little scary at first, but once you have learned to stay afloat, you are soon having fun. Well the same is true of seal pups.

Some seal pups can swim within minutes of being born. Others wait a few weeks before taking a dip. Although they are some of nature's most skillful swimmers, a pup may be a bit shocked by its first swim. It wriggles to the water's edge to sniff and watch the water for a little while. Then the pup suddenly takes the plunge. The pup finds it easy to float but it is still flustered by its first experience of being wet. Soon, though, it is twisting and turning as gracefully as its parents. When a pup gets tired in the water, it can take a ride on its mother's back or flippers.

A growing harbor
seal pup watches its
mother catch a fish.

A male hooded seal blows up a bulge at the front of his head to impress the cows.

Time to Go

Seal mothers don't eat anything while they are raising their pups. The cows get gradually thinner and thinner, and sooner or later they have to leave their babies and head back to sea to feed. Some mothers stay with their young for seven or eight weeks. Other mothers leave much earlier than that. Hooded seals, which live around the ice of the Arctic Ocean, can stay with their pups for only four days! If they stayed any longer, the mothers would starve to death.

Another reason for leaving so soon is that cows must find a mate in order to have another pup the following year.

On Their Own

Even though they are just a few days or weeks old, seal pups are able to look after themselves. They have already learned to swim, and most young have large teeth for catching fish. After their mothers leave them, the pups may spend a few days alone on the beach before heading out to sea.

The world is new to these young seals, and they are curious about everything. They soon figure out how to avoid danger and where to find food. However, learning to catch food takes a while for the pups. Most seals are born in the spring, when fish are plentiful. Until they are able to catch enough fish to feed themselves, the pups live off their blubber.

A young harp
seal ventures
underwater for
the first time.

As the breeding season begins, two male gray seals fight over a cow.

Breeding Season

Seals mate a few weeks after the cows have left
their pups. Most types of seals mate in water.
Only gray seals and elephant seals mate on land.
A bull seal will try to mate with as many cows as
possible. He begins to produce a powerful odor
that might smell bad to us, but it is good at
attracting cows. When he meets a cow, the bull
will perform a swimming display to impress her.
If two bulls are attracted to the same cow, they
will fight one another for her.

The bulls of some types of seals set up a
harem, or group of females, on a beach or an ice
floe. The bulls make sure that all other males
stay away from their mates. The males hiss and
snarl at each other, and fights often break out.

Time to Change

Once the breeding season is over, a seal will go back to living its quiet and peaceful life. After the struggle of raising young and then finding a mate, the seal's fur coat has become shaggy and tattered. It is time for the seal to grow a new one.

This process is call **molting**. In most cases, the coat is shed in large pieces. It is not just the hair that falls away but dead skin as well. The seal does not eat while it molts, and it spends most of its time on land. Yet again it relies on its blubber to feed its body.

Molting takes a few weeks. After that the seal is covered in a new coat of long thick hairs. Then at long last the seal is ready to go back into the sea, where it stays until the following spring.

Words to Know

Arctic   The cold, icy region around the
                  north pole.

Blubber   A thick layer of fat under the skin.

Bull   A male seal.

Cow   A female seal.

Harem   A group of adult females that only
                  mate with one male.

Ice floe   Large piece of ice floating on the sea.

Krill   Shrimplike sea animals.

Mate   To come together to produce young.

Migration   A long journey from one place to
                  another to find food, mates, or a
                  place to give birth.

Molt/molting   To shed a coat of fur and replace it with another.

Mottled   A pattern made up of blotches and spots of two or three colors.

Nurse   To drink milk from a mother's body.

Oxygen   The part of the air that is used by the body.

Pinnipeds   A group of animals whose legs are specially shaped as flippers. Seals, sea lions, fur seals, and walruses all are pinnipeds.

Predators   Animals that hunt other animals for food.

Pups   Young seals.

Zoologists   Scientists who study animals.

Find Out More

Books

Becker, J. *Returning Wildlife: The Northern Elephant Seal.*
Farmington Hills, Michigan: KidHaven Press, 2004.

Bonnett Wexo, J. *Seals and Sea Lions.* Zoobooks. Poway,
California: Wildlife Education, Ltd., 2003.

Thomas, P. *Marine Mammal Preservation.* Science of
Saving. Brookfield, Connecticut: Millbrook Press, 2000.

Web sites

Friends of the Elephant Seal
www.elephantseal.org
Lots of facts about the elephant seals of California.

The Seal Conservation Society
www.pinnipeds.org
Information about seals from all around the world.

Index